Aunt Rose Comes to Stuy

A Tom and Holly story

Barbara Mitchelhill

Series Editor: Louis Fidge

GW00786400

Contents

Aunt Rose comes to stay

There was a letter on the mat.
Holly and Tom went to get it.

'Who is this letter from?' said Holly.

Mum said, 'This letter is from Aunt Rose. She wants to come and stay with us.'

'Who is Aunt Rose?' Holly said.

'She is my sister. Look. This is a photo of her,' Dad said.

'Where can she sleep?' Tom said.

Mum said, ' Aunt Rose can have this bedroom. But we must get some new curtains.'

They went to the shop to buy some curtains.
Mum liked the red curtains.
But Holly and Tom liked the pink and
green curtains.

Dad put the new curtains in the bedroom.
The curtains looked good.

'We must get a new chair for Aunt Rose, too,'
Tom said.

They went to the shop to buy a chair.
Dad liked the green and white chair.
But Holly and Tom liked the blue chair.

They put the new chair in the bedroom.
The chair looked good.

'We must get a new quilt for Aunt Rose, too,'
Holly said.

They went to the shop to buy a quilt.
Mum liked the pink quilt.
But Holly and Tom liked the red, white and blue quilt.

Aunt Rose came in her car.

She liked the bedroom.
'The curtains are like my dress.
The chair is like my shoes.
The quilt is like my bag,' she said.

Then Aunt Rose went back to her car.
Holly and Tom went with her.
There were some presents in her car.

'Can we help you carry the presents?' said Tom and Holly.

'Yes, you can. Thank you,' Aunt Rose said.

Holly and Tom helped Aunt Rose carry the presents.

It was very windy.

I think this present is for Mum,'
said Aunt Rose.

'Thank you,' said Mum.

14

'I think this present is for Dad,'
said Aunt Rose.

'Thank you,' said Dad.

'I think this present is for Joe,'
said Aunt Rose.

'Mine! Mine!' said little Joe.

There were two more presents.
'Is this for me?' said Holly.
'Yes, it is,' said Aunt Rose.
'Thank you,' said Holly.
'Is this for me?' said Tom.
'Yes, it is,' said Aunt Rose.
'Thank you,' said Tom.

Mum looked in her box.
'This isn't my present,' she said.

Dad looked in his box.
'This isn't my present,' he said.

Tom looked in his box.
'This isn't my present,' he said.

Holly looked in her box.
'This isn't my present,' she said.

Little Joe looked in his box.
'Chocolate!' he said.

They all laughed!

New car,
Old car,
Yellow car,
Blue car.

New dress,
Old dress,
Pink dress,
Blue dress.

New shoes,
Old shoes,
Green shoes,
Blue shoes.

New box,
Old box,
Hot box,
Cold box.

23

Word list

a	curtains	Joe	present(s)	this
all	Dad	laughed	put	to
and	dress	letter	quilt	Tom
are	for	like	red	too
Aunt	from	liked	Rose	two
back	get	little	said	us
bag	good	look/looked	she	very
bedroom	green	mat	shoes	wants
blue	have	me	shop	was
box	he	mine	sister	we
but	help/helped	more	sleep	went
buy	her	Mum	some	were
came	his	must	stay	where
can	Holly	my	thank you	white
car	I	new	the	who
carry	in	of	then	windy
chair	is	on	there	with
chocolate	isn't (is not)	photo	they	yes
come	it	pink	think	you

Language structures

Past simple tense:
was/were, helped, said, went, liked, put, came, looked, laughed

Wh questions:
Who is Aunt Rose?
Where can she sleep?

must:
We must get a new chair.

can:
Where can she sleep?
Can we help you carry the presents?

but:
Dad liked the green and white chair. But Holly and Tom liked the blue chair.

to be like:
The curtains are like my dress.

want to:
She wants to come and stay with us.

Object pronouns:
me, us, her